Discover & Learn

Living Planet

This book is perfect for pupils studying
KS2 Geography (ages 7-11).

It's jam-packed with facts, diagrams and questions covering
the physical and human aspects of life on planet Earth —
ideal for exploring and understanding the whole topic.

Published by CGP

Consultant: Joanna Copley

Editors: Sharon Keeley-Holden, Sarah Pattison, Rebecca Russell

Reviewer: Alison Griffin

ISBN: 978 1 78294 984 8

With thanks to Mary Falkner for the proofreading.

With thanks to Jan Greenway for the copyright research.

Printed by Elanders Ltd, Newcastle upon Tyne

Clipart from Corel®

Contents

The Solar System

The Solar System is made up of the Sun and the eight planets that move around it. The Earth is one of these planets. Every planet moves around the Sun in a big loop called an orbit. Planets closer to the Sun take less time to orbit (go around) the Sun. Planets further away take much longer. It takes the Earth <u>one year</u> to orbit the Sun.

You can use sentences like these to help you remember the <u>order</u> of the planets:

<u>M</u>ercury, <u>V</u>enus, <u>E</u>arth, <u>M</u>ars, <u>J</u>upiter, <u>S</u>aturn, <u>U</u>ranus, <u>N</u>eptune

<u>M</u>y <u>V</u>ery <u>E</u>lderly <u>M</u>ouse <u>J</u>ust <u>S</u>leeps <u>U</u>nder <u>N</u>apkins

These lines show the <u>orbits</u> of the eight planets in the Solar System.

Fact Sheet: Earth
Type of planet: rocky
Atmosphere: mainly <u>nitrogen</u> and <u>oxygen</u>
(there's more on the atmosphere on page 4)
Average temperature: 15 °C
Time to orbit Sun: 365 days (1 year)

Getting in a spin

The planets don't just orbit the Sun. They're also <u>rotating</u> (spinning) as they go. It might not feel like it, but the ground under your feet is spinning at 600 miles per hour right now. That's as fast as an aeroplane.

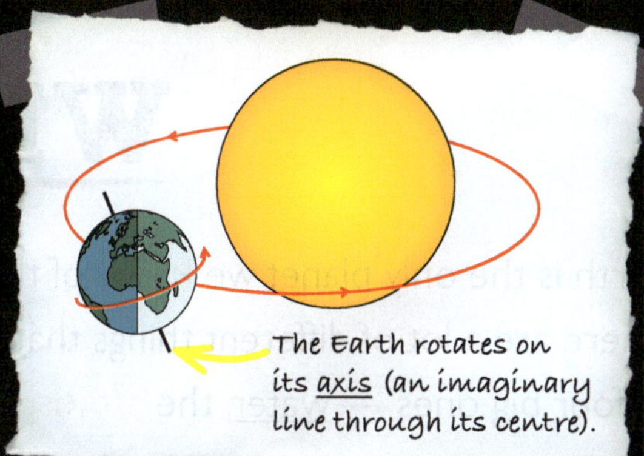

IT'S GOING TO BE A LONG DAY

A day on Earth lasts for <u>24 hours</u> because it takes the planet <u>24 hours</u> to rotate once on its axis. It takes other planets different amounts of time to rotate. One day on Venus is the same length as <u>243 days</u> on Earth.

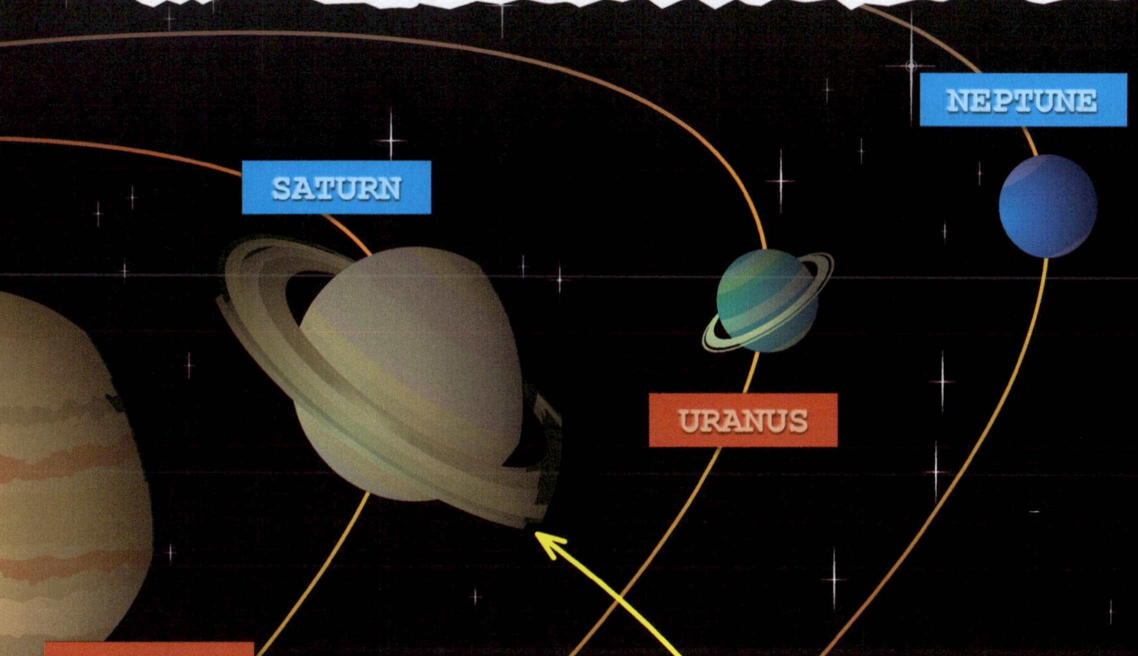

Fact Sheet: Saturn

Type of planet: gas giant (mostly <u>swirling gases</u>, with liquid closer to the centre)

Atmosphere: <u>hydrogen</u> and <u>helium</u> (but as there's no solid surface, the atmosphere blends in to the planet).

Average temperature: -178 °C

Time to orbit Sun: 29 years

Someone's been eating my porridge...

The Earth orbits the Sun in a special place called the Goldilocks Zone. It's not too close or too far from the Sun, so we can live there. In other words, it's not too hot and it's not too cold. It's just right. There's more on why the Earth's just right for us on the next page.

Why Earth?

Earth is the only planet we know of that has <u>life</u> on it. So what makes Earth so special?
There are a lot of different things that mean life can exist on Earth, but we're going to look
at four big ones — <u>water</u>, the atmosphere, <u>warmth</u> and <u>light</u>.

Our safety net

The atmosphere is a thin layer of <u>gases</u> that surrounds the planet.
One of these gases is <u>oxygen</u>, which we need to breathe.

If you looked at the Earth from outer space,
the atmosphere would look like a
<u>pale blue bubble</u> around the planet.

The atmosphere is like a
<u>shield</u> that protects the
Earth from meteors and
harmful radiation.

It also helps to keep
the Earth at the right
<u>temperature</u> for us.

A blue planet

<u>Water</u> is vital to make
a planet <u>suitable</u> to live on.

The Earth is mostly covered with water —
only about <u>one third</u> of the Earth's surface is
<u>land</u>.

Almost all of the water on Earth
is in the <u>oceans</u>. It's also stored
in glaciers, <u>rocks</u> and <u>lakes</u>.

*How many different ways can
you think of that we use water?*

You light up my life

The Earth is the perfect distance from the Sun, so we get the right amount of <u>heat</u> and <u>light</u>.

HEAT

The Sun gives out <u>heat</u> which makes
the Earth warm enough to <u>sustain</u> life.
The <u>atmosphere</u> traps some of this heat
to stop the planet getting <u>too cold</u> at night.

'Life' doesn't just mean humans —
it can be anything from the tiniest
microbe to the biggest whale.

LIGHT

We also need <u>light</u> from the Sun. The plants we use for <u>food</u> use the
light energy for photosynthesis. They couldn't grow without sunlight.

Another reason Earth is so good at supporting life is that it's
never <u>dark</u> for too long. The Earth rotates once every <u>24 hours</u>.
That means each side of the planet gets sunlight <u>often enough</u>
for plants to grow.

MISSION TO MARS

There are plans to have <u>people</u> living on <u>Mars</u>
sometime in the future. Since the atmosphere
on Mars is different from Earth's atmosphere,
people would have to live inside <u>shelters</u> and
wear <u>spacesuits</u> when they went outside.

This is what the shelters might look like
when we finally send people to Mars.

Why do you think it might be a good
idea to be able to live on another planet?

Is there anybody out there?

A planet needs the perfect atmosphere and temperature, as well as light and water, to be
suitable to live on. If one of these things isn't right, life can't exist. That might be why we
haven't found any other planets with life yet — because a lot of them just aren't right.

What Time Is It?

The Earth completes one rotation every 24 hours. When it's light outside, our part of the world is facing the Sun. When it's dark outside, our part of the world has turned away from the Sun.

Another place, another time

It can't be daytime everywhere on Earth at the same time, because the whole of the Earth can't face the Sun at the same time. This means when it's daytime on one side of the world, it's night-time on the opposite side.

When you go to bed tonight, there will be people in other countries eating their lunch, sitting in class or just waking up. That's because it's not the same time everywhere in the world.

No matter where they live, everyone wants 12 pm (noon) to be the middle of the day for them. This means different places on Earth need to have their own time zones.

Getting in the zone

Each blue line on this map separates the world's time zones — each 'zone' is an hour apart. The lines are more or less straight, but sometimes they have to wiggle about so that whole countries can be in the same time zone.

At the bottom of the map you'll see the times in different zones when it's 12 noon in the UK.

Can you spot a country that has more than one time zone?

A land before time

In the past, each town in the UK used the position of the Sun to tell the time. That meant it was a slightly different time in every town, which became too confusing when people started to travel more.

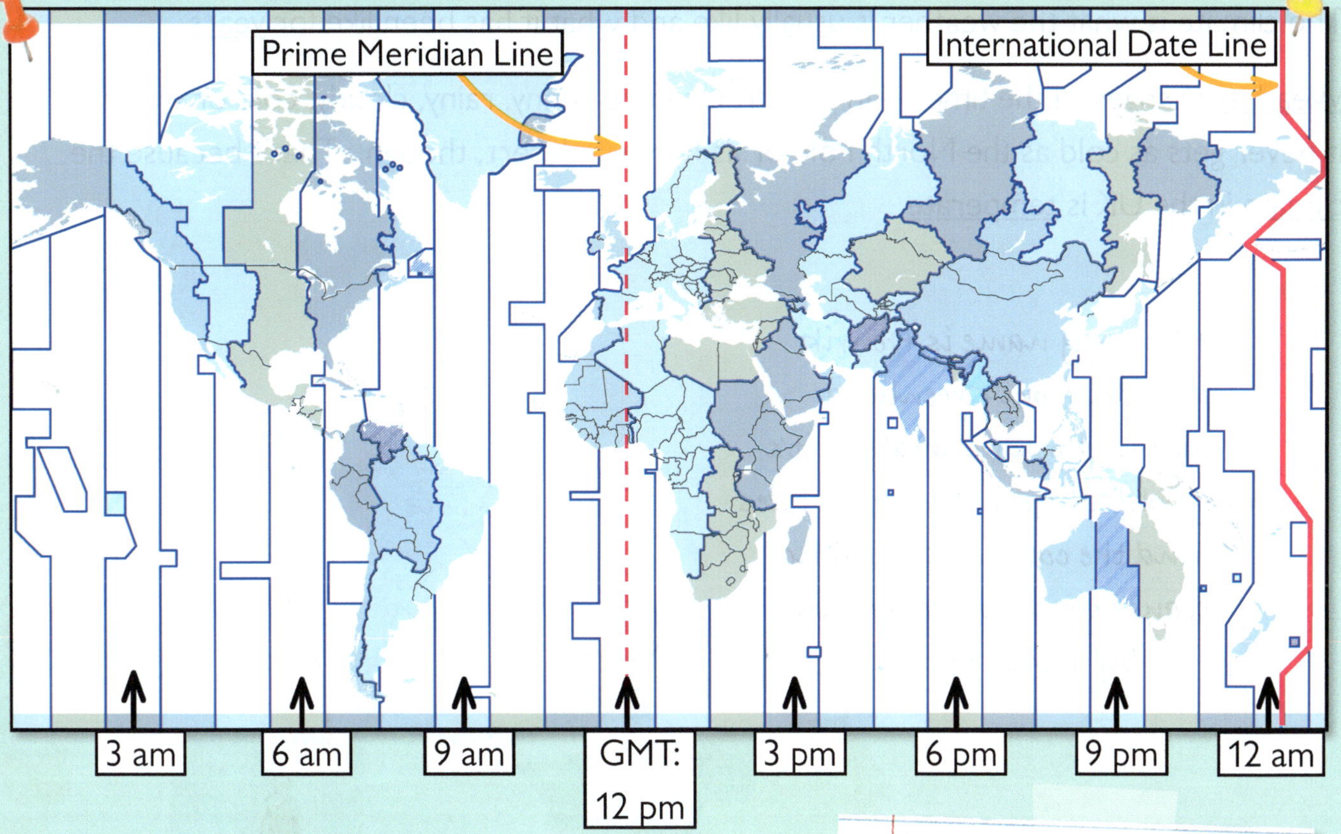

They decided to choose one standard time that everyone would use — the time at the Royal Observatory in Greenwich, London. This is called Greenwich Mean Time (GMT).

The imaginary north-south line through Greenwich is called the Prime Meridian Line and it's used as the basis for our time zone system.

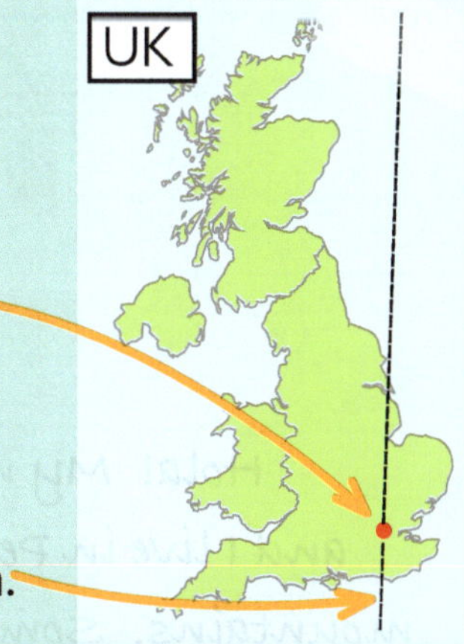

You can be a time traveller...

The International Date Line is exactly half way around the world from the Prime Meridian Line. It marks the point where one day ends and the next one begins. If you stand on the west side of the line and then cross over it, you will go back in time by 24 hours.

More Than Weather

The world can be split up into <u>zones</u> depending on the climate you would find there. Climate and weather are not the same thing, but they are <u>related</u>.

The climate is what the weather is <u>usually like</u> and what it has been like for <u>years</u>.

<u>Weather</u> changes all the time — in the UK it can be sunny, rainy, cloudy, cold or warm. It never gets as cold as the North Pole or as hot as a desert, though. That's because the <u>climate</u> in the UK is <u>temperate</u>.

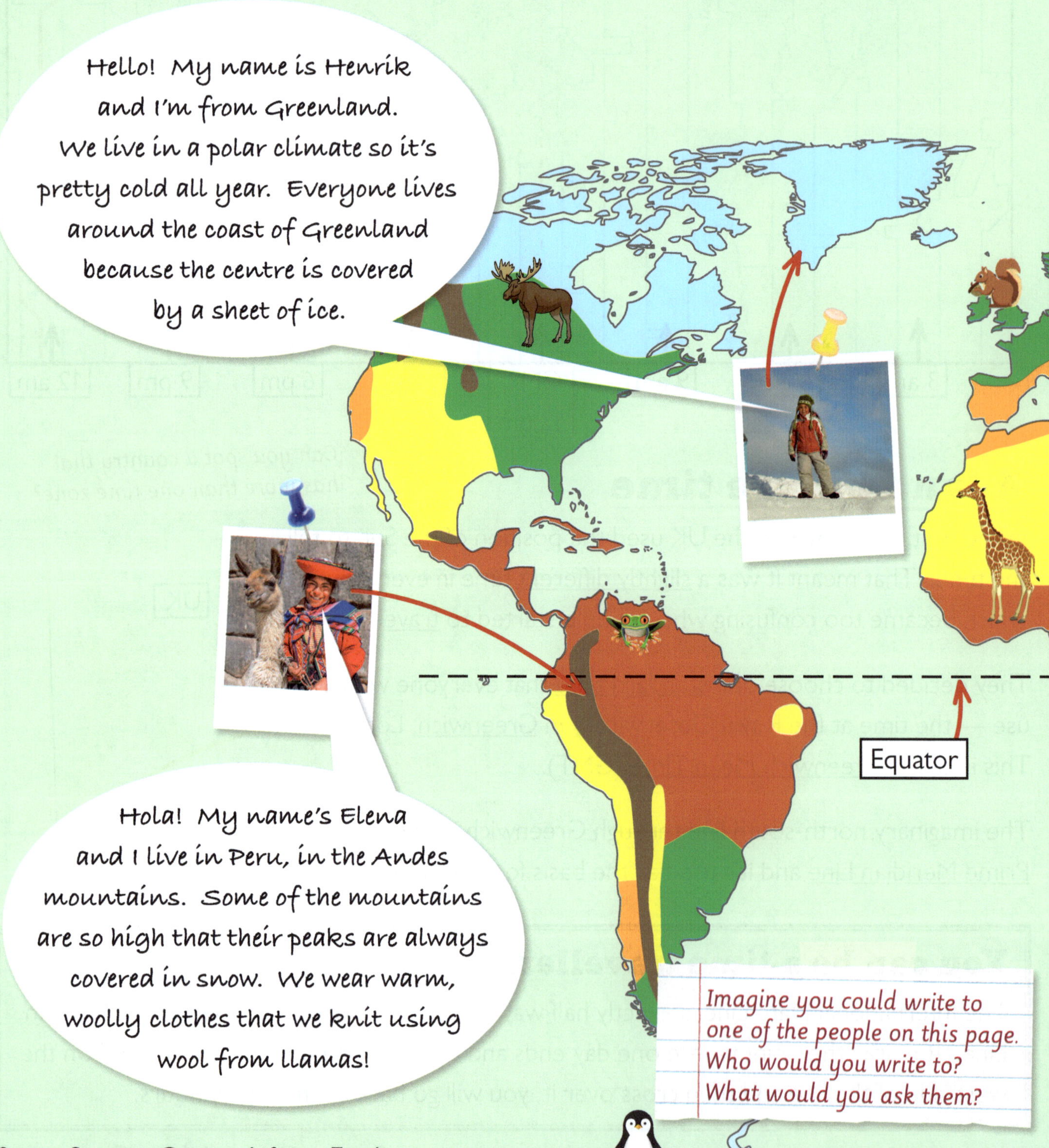

POLAR — Very <u>cold</u> and <u>dry</u> all year. Found in areas around the North and South Poles.

MEDITERRANEAN — <u>Mild winters</u> and dry, <u>hot summers</u>. Found mainly around the Mediterranean Sea.

TEMPERATE — <u>Cold</u> winters and <u>mild</u> summers. Found in the UK.

TROPICAL — <u>Hot</u> and <u>wet</u> most of the year. Found around the <u>equator</u>, where <u>rainforests</u> grow.

DESERT — <u>Dry</u> all year. Some deserts are <u>very hot</u> all year, others have <u>really cold winters</u>. Also known as an 'arid' climate.

ALPINE — <u>Very cold</u> all year. Found in high, mountainous areas.

Worlds apart...

The climate affects the plants and animals that live in a certain place. It can also affect the houses people live in, the jobs they do and the clothes they wear.

Ocean Life

There are five oceans — the Arctic, Atlantic, Pacific, Indian and Southern.
They're all connected together and contain <u>almost all</u> of the water in the <u>world</u>.

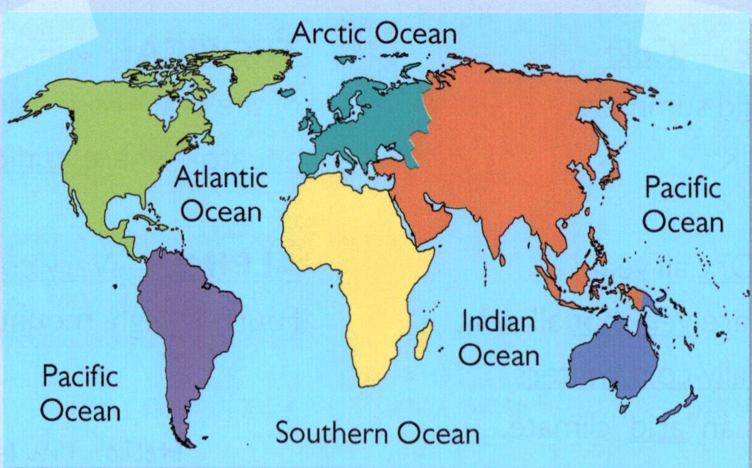

Way down deep

As you go deeper into the ocean, the <u>temperature</u> and the <u>light</u> levels both fall.

SUNLIGHT ZONE

The Sun provides <u>warmth</u> and <u>light</u> for this layer, so many species of plants and animals can live here. The Sunlight Zone is the <u>smallest</u> ocean zone, but it contains <u>most</u> of the <u>life</u> in the ocean. You'll find seaweed, sharks, dolphins, seals, whales, eels and much more here.

TWILIGHT ZONE

This zone gets a <u>little</u> sunlight, but not enough for plants to survive.
The animals that live here feed on <u>plant matter</u> that has fallen
from the Sunlight Zone above, or they eat <u>other animals</u>.

MIDNIGHT ZONE

This zone gets absolutely <u>no sunlight</u>. It's very <u>cold</u> and very <u>dark</u>.
Plants can't live here, but a few animals can. The animals that live
here are some of the <u>weirdest</u> and most <u>mysterious</u> in the world.

Hide and seek

Animals and plants have adapted to live almost anywhere — some animals can even live in the toughest environments like the bottom of the ocean. The adaptations of ocean animals depend on which zone of the ocean they live in. These special features make them better at finding food, communicating, or escaping from predators.

SEAWEED

Adaptation: Air bladders

Effect: These bubbles of air help some types of seaweed to float on the top of the ocean. Like all plants, seaweed needs sunlight to live. This way it can get all the light it needs.

SHARK

Adaptation: Camouflage (blending in with the surroundings)

Effect: A shark's dark back blends in with the dark sea below and its lighter belly blends in with the sunlit water above. This helps the shark to catch its prey without being seen.

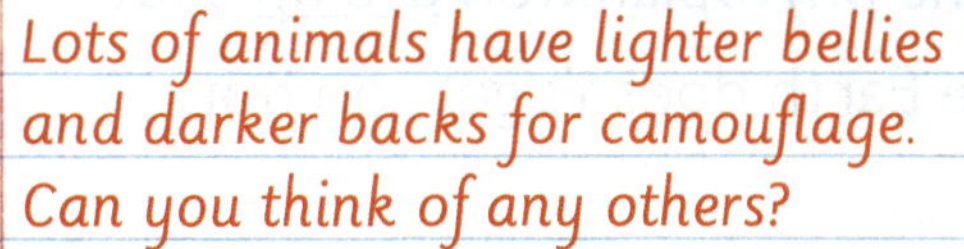

Lots of animals have lighter bellies and darker backs for camouflage. Can you think of any others?

FIREFLY SQUID

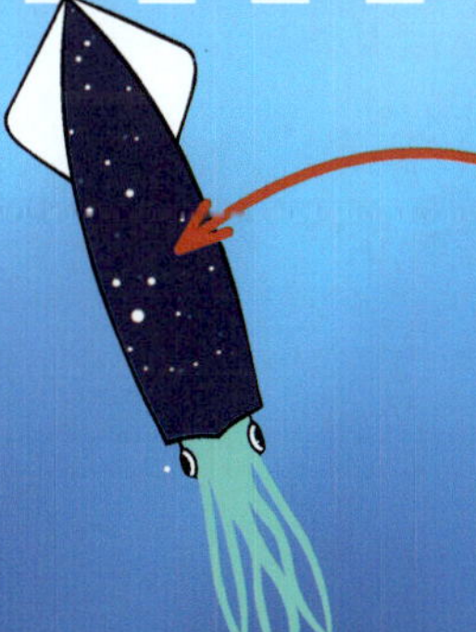

Adaptation: Bioluminescence (producing light)

Effect: Firefly squid use their glow-in-the-dark spots to communicate with other squid in the low light of the Twilight Zone. They also use them to attract small fish, which they eat.

ANGLERFISH

Adaptation: Bioluminescence

Effect: Anglerfish use a light on their head like a fishing rod to attract small fish. Their light also means they can see to eat them.

Oceans and the Climate

On pages 4 and 5 we saw how important the atmosphere is. It keeps our planet warm and contains <u>oxygen</u> which we need to breathe. The oceans do these things too, but in a different way. We need the atmosphere <u>and</u> the oceans to live on Earth.

Breathe in that sea air

<u>Phytoplankton</u> are tiny plants that live in the ocean. <u>Carbon dioxide</u> from the air <u>dissolves</u> in the ocean and is taken in by phytoplankton. They turn it into <u>oxygen</u> during photosynthesis. There are thousands of phytoplankton in a single drop of sea water, so between them they release a lot of oxygen, which we need to <u>survive</u>.

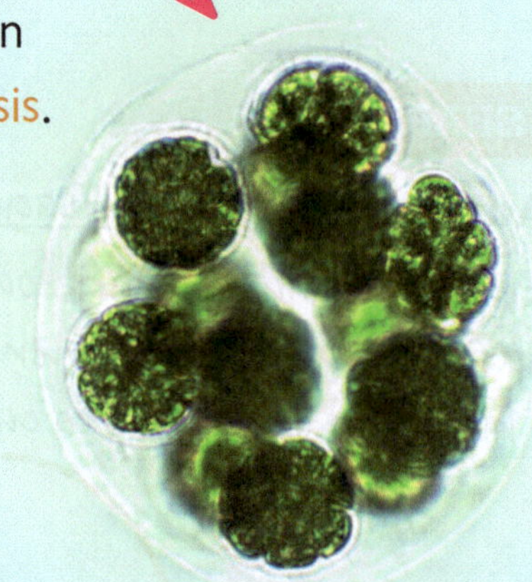

They also help keep the Earth's <u>temperature</u> right. Too much carbon dioxide in the atmosphere can cause the Earth to <u>heat up</u>. The phytoplankton <u>use up</u> a lot of carbon dioxide so the Earth doesn't get too hot.

Phytoplankton are usually too small to see without a microscope, but if there are lots of them, they can turn the water <u>green</u>.

There are so many phytoplankton in the ocean that you can sometimes even see them from space!

Current events

The oceans soak up <u>heat</u> from the Sun, and <u>transport</u> it all around the world. This means that most of the world is warm enough to live in. Warm and cold water travels around the world in pathways called <u>currents</u>. These currents are caused by <u>wind</u> and the <u>rotation</u> of the Earth.

STREAM ON

The <u>current</u> that passes right next to the UK is known as the <u>Gulf Stream</u>.
It carries <u>warm water</u> from tropical regions to the north of Europe.
The warm water heats up the air above it. This warmed air then blows
over the UK, stopping it from getting <u>too cold</u> in winter.

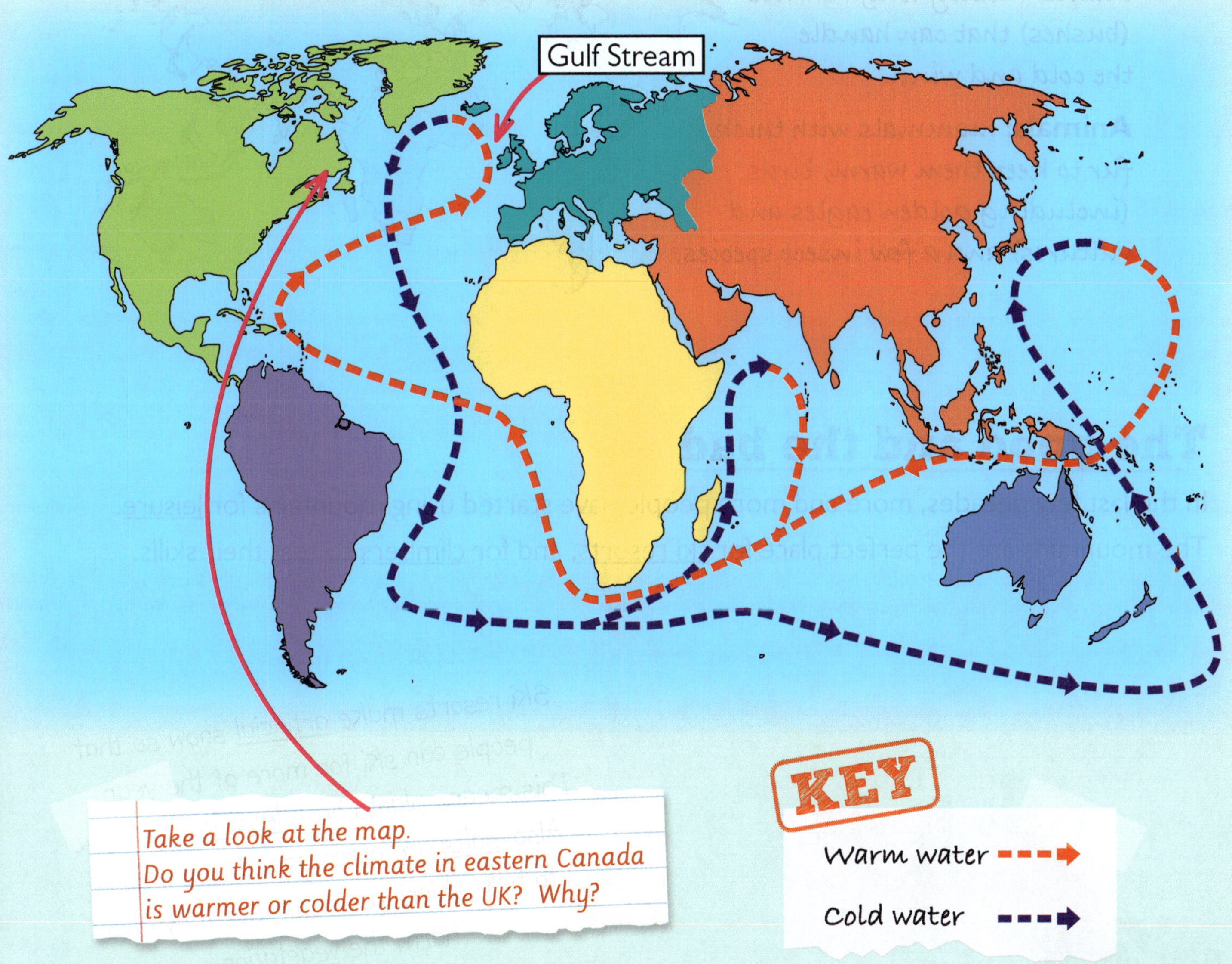

Take a look at the map.
Do you think the climate in eastern Canada
is warmer or colder than the UK? Why?

Never–ending motion...

The currents shown on the map are surface currents. The ocean has huge underwater currents, too. In some places, the water moves from the bottom of the ocean to the top. In other places, it falls to the bottom. This mixes the water in the different ocean layers.

Mountains

A biome is an area with certain plants and animals that have <u>adapted</u> to the climate there. <u>Alpine biomes</u> can be found high in the mountains all over the world.

Fact Sheet: Alpine Biomes

Location: North America, South America, Asia, Europe.

Climate: Alpine climate — cold, windy and snowy all year.

Plants: mostly tough shrubs (bushes) that can handle the cold and wind.

Animals: mammals with thick fur to keep them warm, birds (including golden eagles and vultures) and a few insect species.

The good and the bad

In the last few decades, more and more people have started using mountains for <u>leisure</u>. The mountains are the perfect place for <u>ski resorts</u>, and for <u>climbers</u> to test their skills.

Ski resorts make <u>artificial</u> snow so that people can ski for more of the year. This means plants have <u>less time</u> to grow. Also, <u>salts</u> are often added to the snow to help skiers go faster, but they also harm the <u>vegetation</u>.

Building things like <u>hotels</u> and <u>roads</u> causes animals to lose their habitats.

Welcome to the Himalayas

The Himalayas form an enormous <u>mountain range</u> that passes through Nepal, India, Bhutan, China and Pakistan. It's home to the highest mountain in the world — Mount Everest. The animals and plants that live here have <u>adapted</u> to a very <u>cold</u> and <u>windy</u> climate.

<u>Snow leopards</u> have very <u>thick fur</u> to keep them warm. They use their <u>bushy tail</u> to cover their nose and mouth when it's very cold. They also have <u>big paws</u> to help them walk on the snow.

Snow leopard

A tahr is a type of wild goat. They have thick, woolly fur to protect them against the cold. Their <u>strong hooves</u> help them to climb the steep, rocky mountains. They can eat the <u>tough</u>, <u>woody</u> plants found in alpine biomes.

Tahr

Plants like <u>juniper bushes</u> can grow on <u>rocky ground</u>. They are tough and don't usually grow very tall, meaning they won't get blown over by the <u>strong alpine winds</u>.

Juniper

People can adapt too...

The further up a mountain you go, the less oxygen is in the air. For most of us, this would eventually make us feel tired and ill, but the people in the Himalayas have adapted. They have an increased lung capacity, which means they can live there with no problems at all.

Tropical Rainforests

Fact Sheet: Tropical Rainforests

Location: South America, Africa, Asia.

Climate: Tropical — hot and wet most of the year.

Plants: Thousands of different trees and plants that grow close together.

Animals: Millions of different species, including jaguars, parrots, tarantulas, monkeys, gorillas, snakes, frogs and insects.

The rainforest has four layers. The top layer gets the most sunlight, while the bottom layer only gets a little.

What other differences do you think there will be between the forest floor and the emergent layer?

People and the rainforest

This biome produces many different types of <u>food</u>, such as chocolate, bananas and tea. It also provides us with many other <u>resources</u> that we use every day, like <u>wood</u> and <u>paper</u>.

Sadly, the rainforest is being <u>destroyed</u>. Trees are cut down for wood and to make space to <u>graze cattle</u> and <u>grow crops</u>. This has led to some animals becoming endangered.

However, these <u>land use changes</u> provide <u>jobs</u> for local people in farming, logging and road building. Also, selling resources makes <u>money</u> for the country which can be spent on things like <u>hospitals</u> and <u>schools</u>.

A world of its own

Madagascar is an <u>island</u> off the coast of Africa. There's a long strip of <u>rainforest</u> along the east of this country. This rainforest is <u>special</u> because most of the animals and plants <u>don't exist</u> <u>anywhere else</u> in the world.

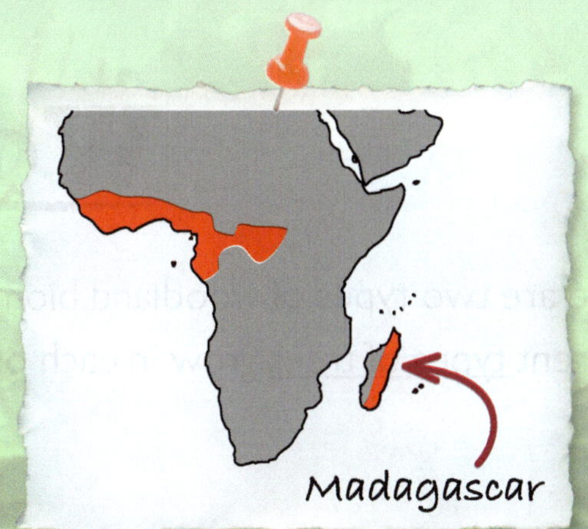

These animals have all <u>adapted</u> to their environment.

Lemur

Lemurs have <u>strong hands</u> and <u>feet</u> to help them grab onto branches as they leap through the trees of the understorey. They also have long tails which they use to help them <u>balance</u> as they climb.

Chameleon

Half of the world's chameleon species live on Madagascar. Chameleons can move each of their eyes in a different direction to keep a look out for <u>predators</u> and <u>prey</u>.

Chameleons are known for their ability to change colour. However, this isn't usually to blend into their surroundings — it's to show other chameleons how they're <u>feeling</u>.

Mantella

The mantella is a type of frog that lives on the <u>forest floor</u> and eats insects. Its bright yellow and black colouring tells predators that it's <u>poisonous</u> and they shouldn't eat it.

Can you think of any more yellow and black animals? Do you think they use these colours as a warning?

Row, row, row your boat...

Scientists reckon that many of the animals that live on Madagascar probably swam there or accidentally drifted there on bits of wood millions of years ago. Since then, they have adapted to help them survive in their rainforest environment.

Woodlands

There are two types of woodland biomes — <u>coniferous</u> forest and deciduous forest. Different <u>types of trees</u> grow in each of these biomes, and the climates are a bit different too.

Fact Sheet: Coniferous Forests

Main locations: North America, Europe, Asia.

Climate: Polar and temperate

Plants: Evergreen trees like pines and spruces. These trees have <u>needles</u> instead of leaves.

Animals: Brown bears, squirrels, owls, wood ants.

Fact Sheet: Deciduous Forests

Main locations: North and South America, Europe, Asia.

Climate: Temperate

Plants: Broad-leaved trees that lose their leaves in winter, e.g. beech and oak.

Animals: Deer, foxes, porcupines, squirrels, mice, owls, doves, moths.

Wild, wild woods

Most of the forests you've been in probably didn't have tigers wandering around in them, but the forests in <u>East Asia</u> do.

The climate here is <u>temperate</u>, so this biome has four clear <u>seasons</u> — spring, summer, autumn and winter.

The trees are <u>deciduous</u>, so the leaves change colour and fall from the trees in the <u>autumn</u>.

The animals in this biome have <u>adapted</u> to suit their surroundings.

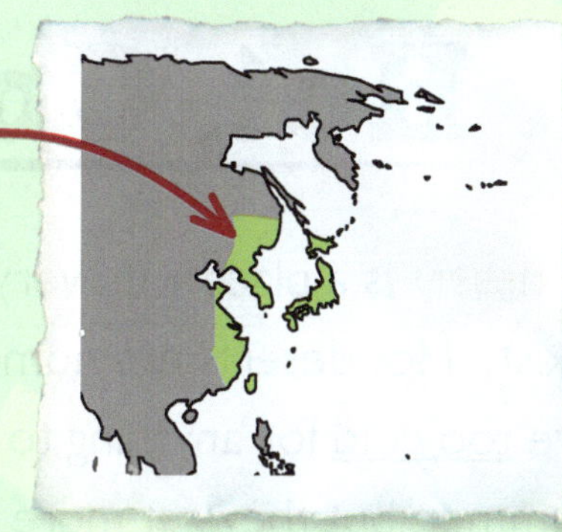

Like most birds of prey, <u>eagles</u> have amazing <u>vision</u>. This helps them spot small prey, like mice and rabbits, from far away, even amongst all the trees.

<u>Tigers</u> have <u>orange and black</u> fur to help them <u>blend</u> in with the forest around them so they can sneak up on their prey. Their stripes match the shadows and branches of the forest.

Chipmunks hibernate in their burrows all <u>winter</u>, waking up every few days for a quick <u>snack</u>. They spend the <u>autumn</u> collecting food for these winter snacks.

If you could have one of these three adaptations, which one would you choose? Why?

Ancient forests...

The UK countryside isn't in its natural state. Long ago, it was covered with forests full of predators like bears, wolves and lynx. But the forests were chopped down to make space for farms and the predators were hunted to extinction to protect farm animals like sheep.

Hot, Cold and In-Between

A desert is a place with very low rainfall. Most deserts are hot, but polar (cold) deserts also exist. Hot deserts are home to many specially adapted plants and animals, but polar deserts are too cold for anything to live there. Mediterranean biomes are similar to hot deserts in summer, but they get more rain in winter.

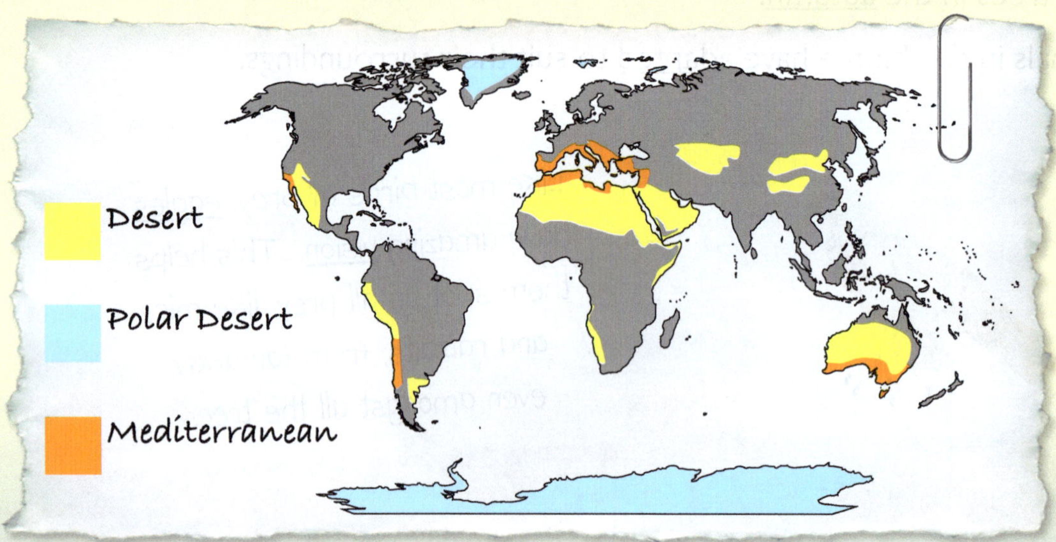

Fact Sheet: Hot Desert

Location: North America, South America, Africa, Asia, Australia.

Climate: Desert

Plants: Tough plants like cacti and shrubs.

Animals: Small mammals, reptiles and birds that have adapted to cope with the very hot and dry conditions.

Fennec foxes sleep in underground dens to keep out of the hot sun. Their big, bat-like ears allow their body heat to escape, helping them to stay cool in the hot weather.

Cacti have long roots that spread far out underground to help them collect water from a large area. They can store a lot of water in their thick stems.

Leopard geckos use camouflage to hide from predators by blending in to the sand and rock. Unlike most geckos, they have claws to help them run across the sand.

Next door neighbours

Mediterranean biomes are usually found next to desert biomes and near the <u>sea</u>.

Fact Sheet: Mediterranean

Location: North America, South America, Europe, Australia

Climate: Mediterranean

Plants: Evergreen fruit trees like <u>orange</u> trees and <u>olive trees</u>. <u>Grasses</u> and <u>shrubs</u> that can survive without much water.

Animals: Nocturnal mammals, reptiles, birds.

COYOTES

Coyotes are <u>nocturnal</u>, so they sleep all day and go outside at night when it's much cooler. Their greyish-brown fur helps them <u>blend in</u> with the dry, bushy landscape around them.

RED ADMIRAL BUTTERFLIES

In summer, these butterflies migrate from Mediterranean biomes to <u>cooler</u> places (like the <u>UK</u>) to lay their eggs. The butterflies that result from the <u>eggs</u> migrate to the <u>Mediterranean</u> before it gets <u>too cold</u>.

Sun seekers

Mediterranean biomes are very popular with <u>tourists</u> because of the warm climate and their location by the <u>sea</u>. A lot of the Mediterranean <u>coast</u> in Europe has been turned into tourist resorts with large roads, hotels and restaurants. Unfortunately, all these new constructions and people can destroy the habitats of lots of species and cause them to become <u>endangered</u>.

Is it hot in here?

The combination of hot and dry weather means that fires can start very easily in a Mediterranean biome. Some plants, like Mediterranean Cypress trees, have adapted to be fire resistant. People are experimenting with planting them to stop wildfires spreading.

Grasslands

Grasslands can be found all over the world. They can be temperate or tropical.
An area of tropical grassland is usually called a savannah.

Fact Sheet: Savannah

Location: South America, Africa, Australia.

Climate: Tropical savannah climate — hot all year and split into two distinct seasons — the wet season and dry season.

Plants: Clumps of grasses and a few trees.

Animals: Wild dogs, cheetahs, elephants, giraffes, grass-eating animals like antelopes and zebras.

Fact Sheet: Temperate Grassland

Location: North America, South America, Asia.

Climate: Temperate — warm summers, mild winters.

Plants: Grasses, very few trees.

Animals: Grass-eating animals like bison and horses, small rodents, foxes, eagles.

Exotic Africa

The savannah covers a lot of the continent of Africa. It's <u>hot</u> all year round, but it <u>rains</u> heavily for around six months of the year. The rain that falls during the <u>wet season</u> means that a variety of different plants and animals can live here.

The animals have adapted to the open <u>plains</u> of the savannah. They need to keep cool and find food, and prey animals need to escape from predators.

Look at the animals below. Can you name any more animals that live in the African savannah?

There are a lot of <u>herbivores</u> (plant-eaters) in the savannah. Giraffes have very <u>long necks</u> so they can eat from trees and don't have to <u>share</u> the grass.

Antelopes can run very fast for a long time thanks to their <u>strong legs</u>. This can help them escape from predators like cheetahs, which are <u>fast sprinters</u> but <u>tire</u> quickly.

Cheetahs can run at almost 70 mph (that's as fast as a <u>car</u> on a motorway). They have special <u>claws</u> that stop them from slipping while they're chasing their prey.

Elephants flap their <u>big ears</u> to keep themselves cool. They also use their <u>tusks</u> to dig in dry <u>riverbeds</u> to find water during the <u>dry season</u>.

Savannah under threat...

Many of the animals in the savannah are poached (hunted illegally) by people who want their fur, tusks or horns to sell. Rhino horns sell for thousands of pounds. Animals like rhinos, lions and elephants are in danger of becoming extinct because of poaching.

A Frozen Place

Tundra biomes are very cold and don't get much <u>rain</u>. Unlike polar deserts, the <u>ice</u> that covers the ground <u>melts</u> once a year which means plants can live here, and so can animals.

Fact Sheet: Tundra

Location: North America, Northern Europe, Northern Asia.

Climate: Polar — cold and dry all year.

Plants: the ground is <u>frozen</u> for most of the year so nothing can <u>grow</u>. When the surface ice <u>melts</u>, small plants can grow for a little while before it freezes again.

Animals: polar bears, seals, reindeer, Arctic foxes.

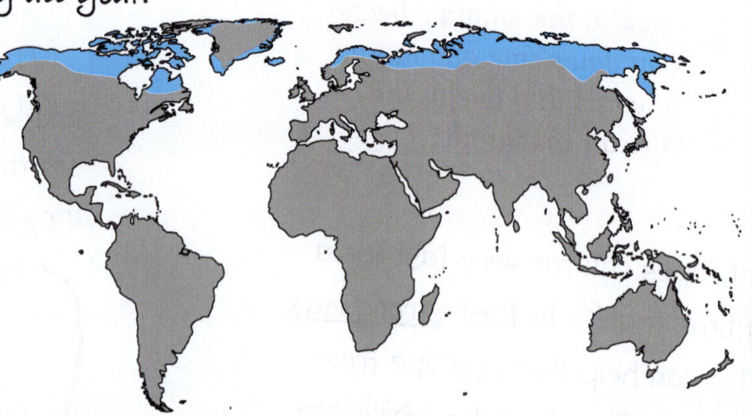

Pipes and night lights

Some tundra biomes have lots of <u>crude oil</u> buried deep underground. This is a <u>natural resource</u> that's used for lots of things like making <u>plastic</u> and <u>fuel</u> for cars. To get this oil, companies build huge <u>pipelines</u> that stretch for hundreds of miles across the tundra. This can affect wildlife like reindeer by stopping them from <u>migrating</u>.

Tourists from all over the world come to tundra biomes hoping to see the <u>Northern Lights</u> — coloured lights that appear in the sky at night near the North Pole.

Northern Lights, Norway

Arctic animals

Life in the frozen tundra can be difficult. The animals that live in the Arctic tundra have developed many <u>different</u> and <u>clever</u> ways to beat the cold.

POLAR BEAR

Adaptation: Thick <u>layers</u> of fur

Effect: Polar bears are able to stay <u>warm</u> even when the temperature is far below freezing (around -40 °C). They have <u>two layers</u> of fur — outer <u>guard hairs</u> and a soft, thick <u>undercoat</u>. The guard hairs are <u>hollow</u> and filled with <u>air</u> to provide <u>insulation</u>. The <u>oil</u> on them <u>repels</u> water and prevents the inner coat <u>getting wet</u> when the polar bear swims.

ARCTIC GROUND SQUIRREL

Adaptation: <u>Hibernation</u>

Effect: Ground squirrels stay <u>warm</u> and <u>safe</u> inside their <u>burrows</u> from September to March. Because they're <u>asleep</u>, they don't need <u>food</u>, which is handy because there isn't very much of it during winter in the tundra.

REINDEER

Adaptation: <u>Migration</u>

Effect: Reindeer move to warmer <u>forest</u> biomes in the winter so that they can find food. They stay there until spring and then return to the tundra. They walk together in large <u>herds</u> for hundreds of miles.

Reducing heat loss is the aim...

Tundra animals usually have smaller ears and noses than animals from warmer biomes. This reduces the amount of their body that's in contact with the freezing Arctic air, meaning they lose less body heat — compare their ears to the fennec fox's ears on p.20.

Water Worlds

There are two main water biomes — the <u>salt water</u> biome and the <u>fresh water</u> biome. These biomes can be divided into many smaller biomes — a <u>coastal</u> biome is an example of a type of salt water biome.

Where the land meets the sea

The land doesn't suddenly stop when the sea starts. It continues <u>under</u> the sea until it reaches the <u>deep ocean</u>. This part of the land is called the continental shelf.

The <u>coastal biome</u> includes the continental shelf and the water <u>above</u> it, as well as all the land that's covered by the sea during <u>high tide</u>.

This biome gets lots of <u>sunlight</u> so many plants and animals live here. Kelp (seaweed) forests, coral reefs, fish, dolphins, sharks and octopuses are just some of the wildlife you might see.

Marine mangroves

Mangroves are special trees that can grow in <u>tropical</u> coastal biomes.

They could grow happily in <u>fresh water</u>, but growing in salt water means they don't have much <u>competition</u> from other plants and get all the space to themselves.

The underwater <u>roots</u> make the perfect home for fish and other ocean creatures. They can find <u>food</u> here and also hide from <u>predators</u>.

Fantastic Fens

A <u>wetland</u> biome is a <u>flat</u> area covered in <u>shallow</u> water.

Wetland biomes can be <u>salt water</u>, <u>fresh water</u> or a <u>mixture</u> of the two.

The Fens (or Fenlands) are an area of <u>fresh water</u> wetland in the East of England.
The Fens are full of plants like <u>grasses</u> and <u>sedges</u>. Many <u>wading birds</u>, <u>insects</u>
and <u>mammals</u> make their home here too.

Bitterns are a type of <u>wading</u> <u>bird</u> that like the shallow water. When they want to hide, they stand very still with their beaks pointing <u>upwards</u> and pretend to be a <u>plant</u> — their <u>stripy</u> feathers help them blend in with the grasses.

Water lilies have large, <u>flat leaves</u> that float on top of the water to catch as much <u>sunlight</u> as possible. Their flowers are shaped like <u>bowls</u> to help them float.

DEFENDING THE FENS

In the 1600s, people started <u>draining</u> the Fens to make more room for <u>farmland</u>. The land was perfect for farming because it was so <u>fertile</u>, but this meant lots of animals lost their habitats.

In 2003, a project was started to <u>flood</u> some of the drained areas and bring back the plants and animals that used to live there.

Going... going... gone?

In the last 100 years, the world has lost more than half of its wetlands. That's because people think the land would be more useful as something else, like farmland. Wetlands are actually home to thousands of animals and plants that need the water to survive.

Making Changes

Everyone needs resources such as food, water and materials to build homes with. But when too many people use too many resources, it causes problems.

Settling down

The Ancient Egyptians settled along the River Nile 7,000 years ago. Most of Egypt is a desert, but near the river, people were able to get drinking water and grow crops.

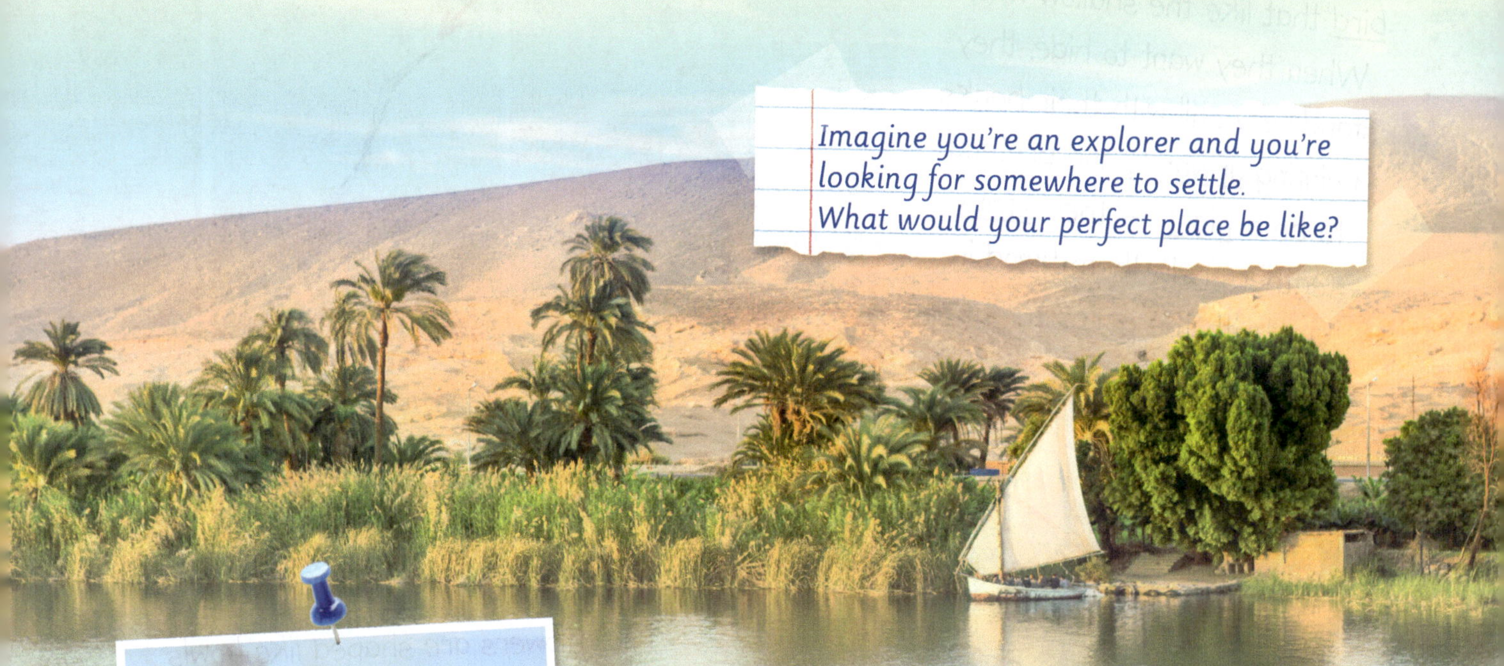

Imagine you're an explorer and you're looking for somewhere to settle. What would your perfect place be like?

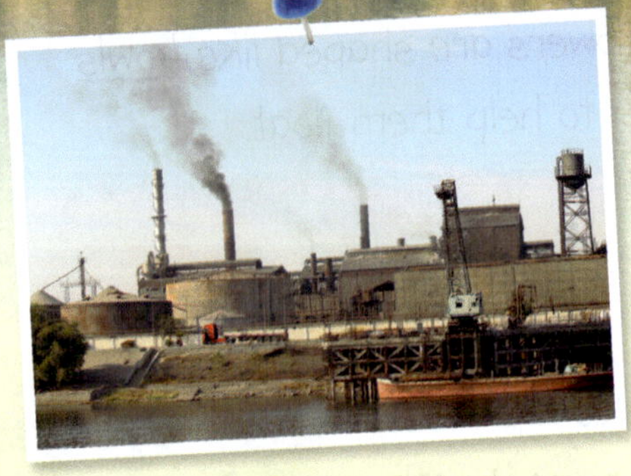

People still grow crops along the banks of the Nile, but today they use chemical fertilisers and pesticides which wash into the Nile. Plastic and sugar factories also pollute the river with waste.

Changed days

Today, we don't all need to live around rivers. We can get lots of the things we need from greater distances away thanks to transport and technology. Clean water comes to our houses through pipes, and a lot of food in the supermarkets comes from all over the world.

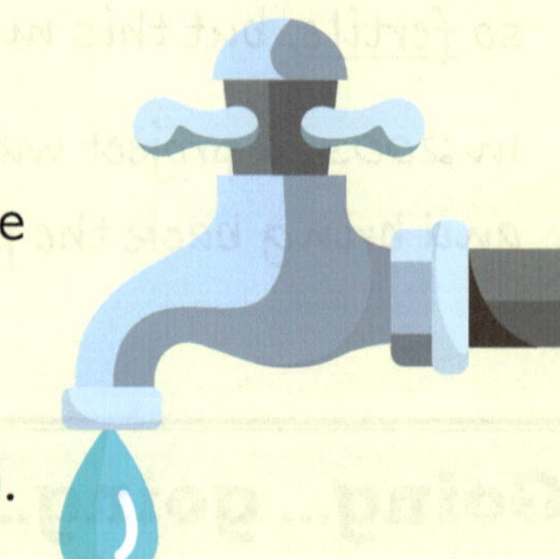

These days, there are also a lot more people on Earth — over 8 billion in fact. This many people use a lot of resources and produce a lot of waste.

Doing damage

Many of the products we use every day add to environmental problems.
Think about a packet of crisps...

<u>Palm oil</u> is an ingredient in almost half the food we buy
— including crisps. It comes from <u>oil palm trees</u> that
grow in <u>tropical</u> conditions.

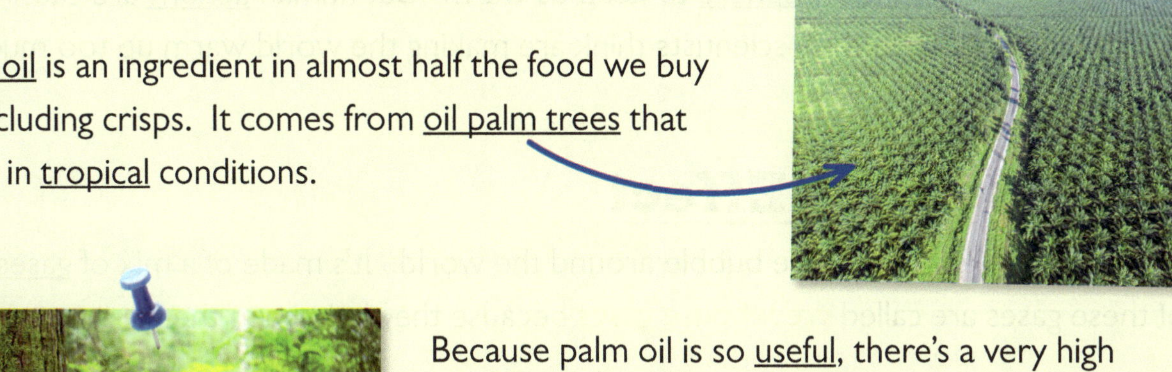

Because palm oil is so <u>useful</u>, there's a very high
<u>demand</u> for it. More and more of the <u>rainforest</u> is being
<u>burned down</u> to make room for more palm oil fields.

Animals that live in the rainforest, like <u>orangutans</u>, are
now <u>endangered</u> because so much of their <u>home</u> has been
destroyed for palm oil.

Polluting plastics

Back to that packet of crisps. The packet itself is actually made of layers of <u>plastic</u>.
<u>Plastic waste</u>, like crisp packets and <u>straws</u>, can't be <u>recycled</u> so they'll end up in a landfill site.
They can also get blown into the <u>ocean</u>,
where they can <u>pollute</u> the water
and hurt the animals.

Can you think of any ways
we could use less plastic?
What about at home?
Or in the supermarket?

What a waste...

About half the plastic that's made every year only gets used once, then it's thrown away.
If you weighed how much plastic is dumped into the ocean every year, it would weigh the
same as 2 million elephants, or 900,000 Tyrannosaurus rexes. That's a lot.

Climate Change

We rely on the <u>Sun</u> and our <u>atmosphere</u> to keep us warm. But human <u>actions</u> are causing <u>changes</u> in the atmosphere, which scientists think are making the world <u>warm up</u> too much.

The Greenhouse Effect

The atmosphere is like a protective bubble around the world. It's made of a mix of <u>gases</u>. Some of these gases are called greenhouse gases because they help keep the Earth <u>warm</u>.

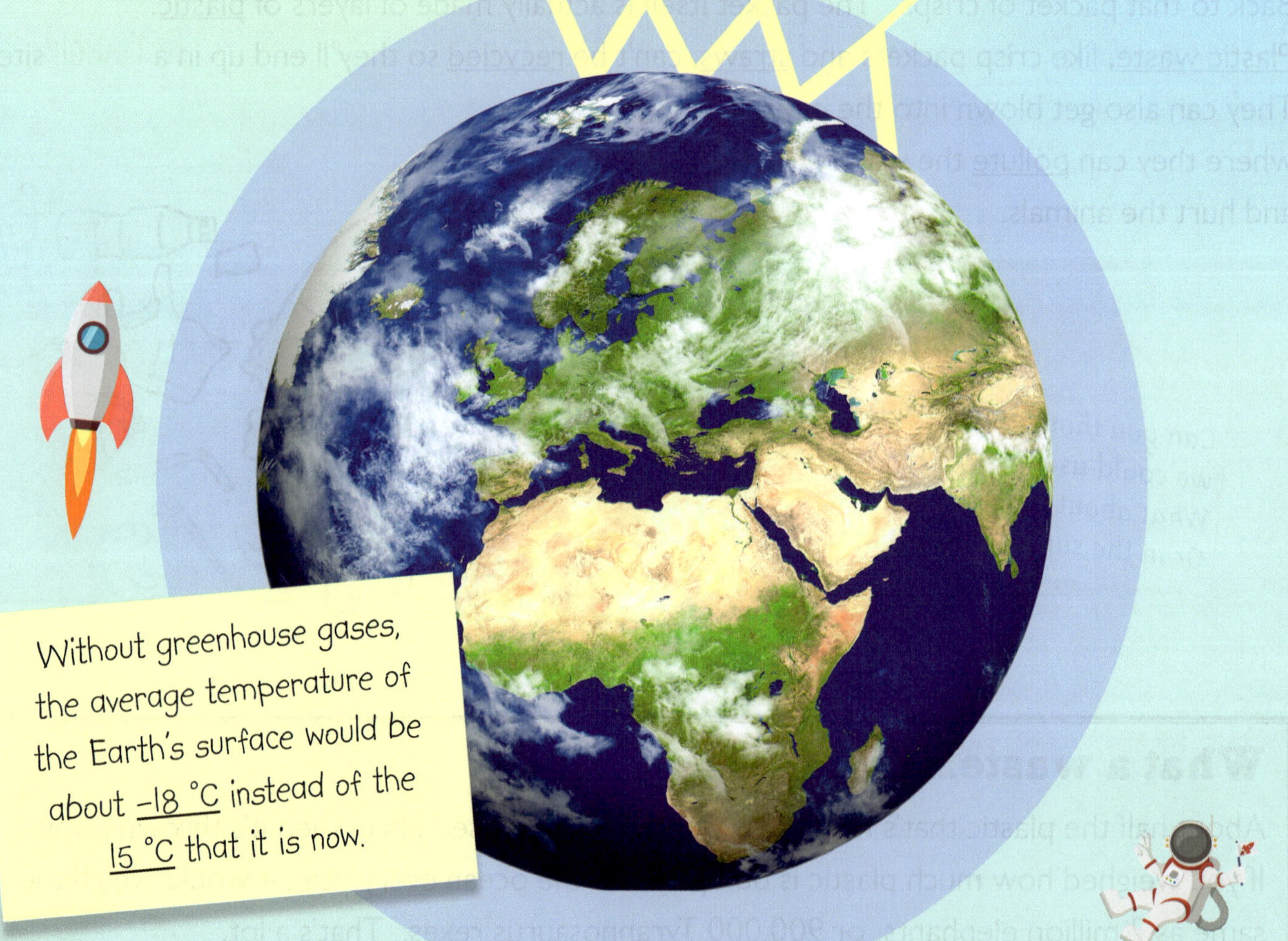

Too much of a good thing

The greenhouse gases in the atmosphere are a <u>good</u> thing — Earth would be too cold for us to live on without them. The trouble is that over the past two hundred years or so, people have been <u>creating</u> a lot of <u>extra</u> greenhouse gases.

The Earth is getting <u>hotter</u>. This is known as <u>global warming</u>. It's thought that <u>humans</u> are causing global warming because the <u>extra</u> greenhouse gases that we create are trapping <u>too much</u> heat in the atmosphere.

WHERE DO GREENHOUSE GASES COME FROM?

Power stations that burn <u>oil</u> and <u>coal</u> to make <u>electricity</u> produce <u>a lot</u> of greenhouse gases. So do <u>cars</u>, <u>planes</u> and <u>agriculture</u> (farming).

The greenhouse gas that people are particularly worried about is carbon dioxide, but there are others too.

Always changing?

Climate change means a <u>long-term</u> change in the <u>weather</u> and <u>temperature</u> of the planet. It can be caused by many things, like <u>volcanic eruptions</u> and changes in the amount of <u>radiation</u> given out by the Sun. The Earth's climate has gone through a lot of changes in the past.

FROZEN PLANET

When <u>woolly mammoths</u> were roaming the Earth, a <u>third</u> of the planet was covered in <u>ice</u>. That's why it was called the <u>Ice Age</u>. There have been at least <u>five</u> ice ages in the Earth's history.

Even though the Earth's climate does change naturally, most scientists agree that humans are <u>forcing</u> the climate to get warmer by putting <u>too many</u> greenhouses gases into the air.

This is having really <u>serious</u> impacts on the world and everything that lives in it, including us.

All about balance...

Plants and trees absorb (suck up) some of the carbon dioxide in the air. But people keep cutting down forests to make room for more factories and farmland. Now we're creating even more carbon dioxide and there are fewer trees to help get rid of it.

Effects of Climate Change

Climate change is a long process — we won't notice a big change overnight.
But <u>rising temperatures</u> are already causing a lot of <u>serious problems</u> all over the world.

Warmer temperatures mean <u>wildfires</u> start and spread more easily.

Extreme weather events, like hurricanes, tornadoes and heat waves, are getting more common.

<u>Droughts</u> (long periods without rain) are more common. Many people struggle to grow <u>food</u> and other crops. Wild animals need to travel further to find food and water, which can bring them into <u>conflict</u> with people.

The ocean <u>absorbs</u> carbon dioxide. This <u>changes</u> the water in the oceans, which can harm ocean creatures.

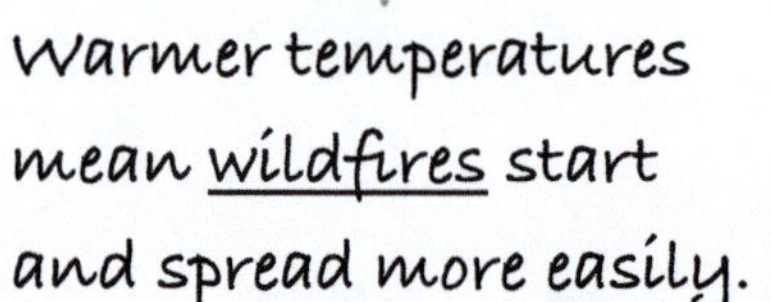

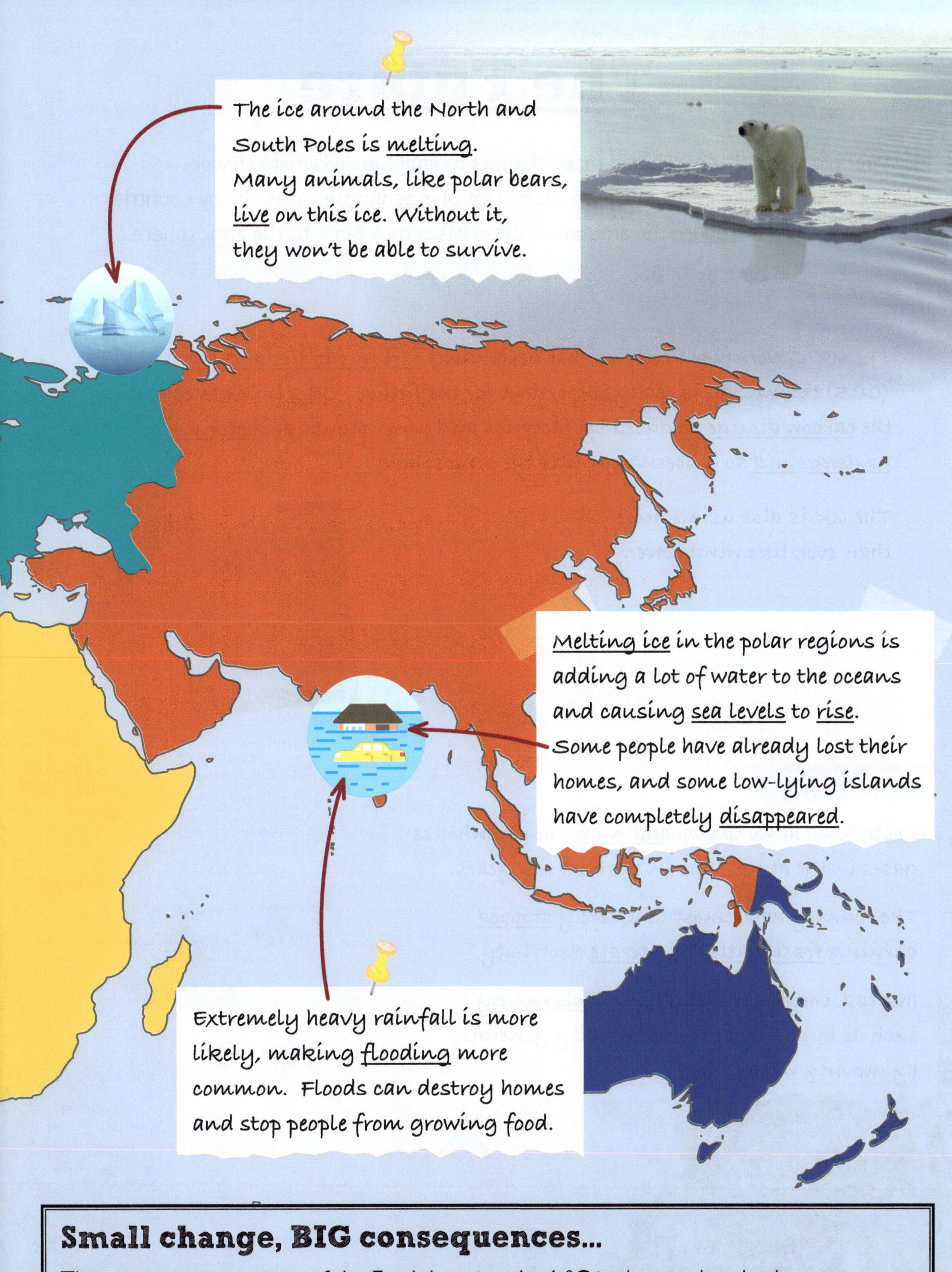

Small change, BIG consequences...

The average temperature of the Earth has risen by 1 °C in the past hundred years. That might not seem like much, but think about how much damage it's done already. But there are ways that we can tackle climate change. Keep reading to find out how...

The Future

Most people agree that we should make changes to limit future climate change. Burning fossil fuels like coal and oil produces a lot of <u>greenhouse gases</u>. Many countries are working hard to <u>reduce</u> the amount of these gases they put into the atmosphere...

THE UK

The UK Government believes that developing <u>carbon capture and storage</u> (CCS) technology is really important for the future. <u>CCS</u> involves collecting the <u>carbon dioxide</u> produced by factories and power plants and <u>storing it</u> <u>underground</u> so it doesn't get into the atmosphere.

The UK is also using more renewable energy than ever, like wind power.

COSTA RICA

Costa Rica aims to stop <u>adding</u> to the greenhouse gases in the atmosphere in the next few years.

The country has almost completely <u>stopped</u> burning <u>fossil fuels</u> to <u>generate</u> electricity.

Instead, they use cleaner, <u>renewable energy</u> such as hydroelectricity (electricity generated by moving water).

What can you do?

Global warming is a <u>big problem</u>, but there are lots of <u>little ways</u> we can help to <u>reduce</u> it. These things all <u>reduce</u> the amount of greenhouse gases put into the atmosphere...

All together now...

We can all do our bit. As well as the steps on this page, some people change their diet — meat and dairy farming produces lots of greenhouse gases, so eating fewer animal products can help limit global warming. If we all work together, we can make a difference.

Glossary

adaptation	A special feature or ability that helps a plant or animal survive in a certain environment.
atmosphere	The layer of gases that surrounds a planet.
biome	An area which has similar plants, animals and climate.
carbon dioxide	A gas found in the atmosphere. Carbon dioxide is a greenhouse gas.
continental shelf	The area at the edge of a continent that's covered by the ocean.
climate	What the weather is usually like and has been like for years.
climate change	Long-term changes in weather and temperature on Earth.
deciduous	Deciduous trees lose their leaves once a year, usually in autumn.
desert	An area that gets very little rain. Deserts can be hot or cold.
endangered	A plant or animal that is at risk of becoming extinct (disappearing forever).
evergreen	Evergreen trees keep their leaves all year.
extinction	When there are no more of a certain animal or plant left in an area, or sometimes no more left anywhere on Earth.
fossil fuel	A fuel made of the remains of plants and animals that were buried millions of years ago. Oil, coal and gas are fossil fuels.
glacier	A large area of thick ice that moves very slowly across the land.
greenhouse gas	A gas in the atmosphere that traps heat from the Sun.
habitat	The place where an animal or a plant normally lives.
hibernate	Spend the winter months sleeping to avoid the cold and lack of food.
humid	When the air is warm and contains a lot of moisture.

hydroelectricity	A type of renewable energy that uses moving water to generate electricity.
landfill	A giant hole in the ground where rubbish is dumped and buried.
meteor	A chunk of rock from outer space that enters our atmosphere. Most meteors burn up in the atmosphere and never hit the ground.
microbe	A tiny form of life, such as a bacterium, that can only be seen with a microscope.
migrate	To move to a different place, usually at a certain time of year.
nocturnal	A nocturnal animal sleeps all day and is active at night.
orbit	The path of an object in space as it travels around another object.
photosynthesis	The process where plants take in water and carbon dioxide and use sunlight to turn it into food and oxygen.
planet	An object in space that orbits the Sun (or another star).
pollute	To make something dirty or unsafe by putting harmful substances into it.
predator	An animal that hunts and eats other animals.
radiation	Energy that something emits (gives out). Heat and light are types of radiation given out by the Sun. Some types of radiation are harmful.
renewable energy	Energy that comes from a source that won't run out, like wind, the Sun or ocean tides.
resource	Things like food, fuel, clothing and building materials that people use.
settle	To make a certain place your home.
Solar System	The Sun, the eight planets and all the smaller objects that orbit the Sun.
species	A group of plants or animals that are similar and can reproduce.
Sun	The star at the centre of the Solar System. The eight planets orbit the Sun.
time zone	A region of the world where everyone uses the same time.

Acknowledgements

Some paragraphs in this book include characters and dialogue which has been invented for dramatic purposes – any similarity to a person, living or deceased, in these areas is merely coincidence.

Graphics used through this book: (push pin) © iStock.com/blackred. (lined paper) © iStock.com/subjug. (torn paper) © iStock.com/ Tolga TEZCAN.

Section One — Life on Earth
p5 (Mars colony) © NASA/Clouds AO/SEArch. p7 (world time zones) © iStock.com / jangeltun. p8 (child from Greenland) © blickwinkel / Alamy Stock Photo. p8 (Peruvian girl) © iStock.com / hadynyah.

Section Two — The Blue Planet
p10 (octopus) © sceka/DigitalVision Vectors/Getty Images, p12 (phytoplankton from space) NASA Ocean Color Web (2018, February) Image Gallery: Gulf of Aden. Accessed March, 2019.

Section Three — Natural Earth
p16 (rainforest) © iStock.com / Bluberries. p27 (bittern) © Krista Lundgren/USFWS. Image licensed under the Creative Commons Attribution 2.0 Generic license.

Section Four — Climate Change
p30 (planet Earth) © JOHN KELLERMAN / Alamy Stock Photo.